So you really want

French

Book One
Answer Book

Published by Galore Park Publishing Ltd
19/21 Sayers Lane, Tenterden, Kent TN30 6BW
www.galorepark.co.uk

Printed by CPI Antony Rowe, Chippenham

ISBN 978 1902984 55 1

First published 2004, reprinted 2009

Details of other Galore Park publications are available at
www.galorepark.co.uk

ISEB Revision Guides, publications and examination papers
may also be obtained from Galore Park.

So you really want to learn

French

Book One
Answer Book

Nigel Pearce B.A. M.C.I.L.

Editor: Joyce Capek

GALORE PARK

www.galorepark.co.uk

Table of contents

Preface

This book contains a complete set of answers to all the exercises in So you really want to learn French Book 1, including translations of all the passages. These answers are not intended to be prescriptive but should provide guidance to those using the course.

Further assessment material to accompany this course is also available, which may be used at the end of each chapter. This material consists of worksheets and audio material, on a single CD, and complements the work of the pupil's book. It has been designed to meet the requirements of pupils preparing for the Common Entrance examination but may prove useful as a means of assessing the progress of anyone using this course. It is available on a multi-format CD (ISBN 978 1902984 62 9), with the worksheets stored in PDF format, allowing users to print off and copy these as required.

NJP, November 2004

Chapitre 1

Bonjour!
Exercice 1.1 – CD:1

Monsieur Béchet.   Hello, Madam!
Madame Lacroix.   Hello, sir!
Monsieur Béchet.   How are you?
Madame Lacroix.   I am fine, thanks. What about you?
Monsieur Béchet.   I am fine.
Robert.   Hello, Nathalie!
Nathalie.   Hello, Robert!
Chantal.   Hello, Nathalie!
Nathalie.   Hi, Chantal! How are you?
Chantal.   I'm fine. What about you?
Nathalie.   I'm really well!

Exercice 1.2 – CD:2

M. Duclerc.   Hello. My name is Monsieur Duclerc.
Pierre.   Hello, sir. My name is Pierre.

Chantal.   Hello, Madam. My name is Chantal.
Mme. Meunier.   Hello, Chantal. My name is Madame Meunier.

Robert.   My name is Robert. What is your name?
Claudine.   Hi, Robert. Me, I'm called Claudine.

Françoise.   My name is Françoise. And you, what is your name?
Nicolas.   I'm Nicolas.
Françoise.   Your name is Nicolas?
Nicolas.   Yes, my name is Nicolas.

Nicolas.   Is she called Claudine?
Françoise.   Excuse me. Is your name Claudine?
Claudine.   Yes, my name is Claudine.

Françoise.   Is he called Charles?
Nicolas.   Excuse me. Is your name Charles?
Robert.   No, my name is Robert.
Nicolas.   No, his name is Robert.

Exercice 1.3 – CD:3

M. Duval.   Hello. My name is Monsieur Duval.
Alexandre.   Hello, sir. My name is Alexandre.

M.Duval. And you, what's your name?.
Aurélie. My name's Aurélie.
M.Duval. What's her name?
Aurélie. She's called Alice.
M.Duval. His name is Jean-Michel, isn't it?
Aurélie. No, sir, he's called Jean-Marc.
M.Duval . So, you're called Alice?
Alice. Yes sir, my name's Alice.
M. Duval. And your name is Jean-Marc?
Jean-Marc. Yes, that's right. I am Jean-Marc. Goodbye sir.
M.Duval. Goodbye, Jean-Marc.

Exercice 1.4

1. regarde
2. passe le CD
3. au revoir
4. il
5. elle

Exercice 1.5

1. Comment dit-on?
2. Elle s'appelle
3. Il s'appelle
4. Bonjour, je m'appelle ...
5. Comment t'appelles-tu?

Exercice 1.6

Pupils will be able to rehearse conversations using what they have learnt from tracks 1 and 2.

Exercice 1.7

(a) Crossword:
     Across:
       1. Bien
       3. Salut

     Down:
       1. Bonjour
       2. Ça va

(c) Any grid which includes all the words given should be acceptable.

Exercice 1.8

A.   Comment t'appelles-tu?
B.   Je m'appelle *x*. Et toi?
A.   Moi, je m'appelle *x*.
B.   Il / elle s'appelle Charles?
A.   Non, il / elle s'appelle *x*.

Exercice 1.9

1.	Il s'appelle Charles	His name is Charles.
2.	Comment tu t'appelles?	What is your name?
3.	Je m'appelle (*x*)	My name is (*x*)
4.	Et toi? Comment tu t'appelles?	And you? What is your name?
5.	Elle s'appelle comment?	What is her name?

Exercice 1.10 – CD:4

My name is Sophie Legrand. I live in Saintes in France. At school I have two friends. They are called Jean and Robert. Robert lives in La Rochelle and Jean lives in Nantes. I also have two girl friends who are called Marie-Claude and Chantal. They (the girls) live in Saintes. And you? Where do you live? Do you live in England?

1.   Sophie habite à **Saintes**.
      Sophie lives in Saintes.

2.   Robert **habite** à La Rochelle.
      Robert lives in La Rochelle.

3.   Sophie a deux amies qui s'appellent **Marie-Claude** et Chantal.
      Sophie has two girlfriends who are called Marie-Claude and Chantal.

4.   Sophie a deux amis **qui s'appellent** Robert et Jean.
      Sophie has two friends who are called Robert and Jean.

5.   Marie-Claude habite à **Saintes**.
      Marie-Claire lives in Saintes.

6.   Jean habite à Nantes et Chantal habite à Saintes.
      Jean lives in Nantes and Chantal lives in Saintes.

7.   Robert habite à La Rochelle.
      Robert lives in La Rochelle.

8.   J'habite à *x*.
      I live in *x (town's name)*.

Exercice 1.11

1.	Calais	8.	La Rochelle
2.	Le Havre	9.	Lyon
3.	Brest	10.	Bordeaux
4.	Rouen	11.	Toulouse
5.	Paris	12.	Avignon
6.	Orléans	13.	Marseille
7.	Nantes	14.	Nice

Les numéros 1-12 - CD:5

The numbers from 1-12 are read out.

Exercice 1.12 - CD:6

1.	Quatre baguettes, s'il vous plaît	Four baguettes, please
2.	Trois pains au chocolat, s'il vous plaît	Three pains au chocolat, please
3.	Huit éclairs, s'il vous plaît	Eight eclairs, please
4.	Trois tartes, s'il vous plaît	Three tartlets, please
5.	Deux gateaux, s'il vous plaît	Two cakes, please

Exercice 1.13

quatre + six, sept + trois, cinq + cinq, huit + deux, neuf + un,
un + neuf, deux + huit, quatre + six, trois + sept.

Vive la France! 1

(a) Robert, Sophie's friend, lives in La Rochelle. La Rochelle is an old and very important port in the history of France. It is also a town (that is) popular with tourists and picturesque.

(b) Students make a wall display of France, using their own experiences from visits they have made and from the internet and tourist offices.

Chapitre 2

La Salle de Classe

Exercice 2.1 - CD 1:7

M. Duclerc. What is there in the classroom?
Nicolas. In the classroom there is a television. There are posters and a computer. There are also a door and a window.
Françoise. There are some tables and a map of France. There are lots of books.
Nicolas. What do you have in your pencil-case?
Françoise. In my pencil-case I have my pencils and my pen. I also have a rubber.
Nicolas. Do you have a ruler?
Françoise. Yes, I also have a ruler.

1. There's a television. There's a computer, posters, a door and a window; there are tables and a map of France. There are lots of books.
2. She has some pencils, a pen, and a rubber. (She also has a ruler.)
3. There are three French words for 'my'. They are: **mon**, used before a masculine noun in the singular (**mon** stylo), **ma**, used before a feminine noun in the singular (**ma** trousse), and **mes**, used before both masculine and feminine nouns in the plural (**mes** crayons).
4. Your pencil case = **ta** trousse. Your pen = **ton** stylo; your pencils = **tes** crayons.

Exercice 2.2

1. le livre
2. la trousse
3. la table
4. les fenêtres
5. l'école
6. le sac
7. la gomme
8. les stylos
9. les règles
10. l'ordinateur

Exercice 2.3

1. ton crayon
2. ton ami
3. ta gomme
4. tes cartes
5. tes profs
6. ton lecteur de CDs
7. ton livre
8. ta trousse
9. tes cahiers
10. ta gomme

Exercice 2.4

1. Mon livre
2. Mon prof
3. Les portes
4. Ma carte
5. Ma trousse
6. Mon stylo
7. Un rétroprojecteur
8. Ma classe
9. Des filles
10. Des garçons

Exercice 2.5 – CD:8

Pierre.   Look! This is my classroom.
Sophie.   In your classroom, is there a whiteboard?
Pierre.   Yes, there is also an overhead projector.
Anne-Marie.   Hi, Pierre. Hi, Sophie.
Pierre.   Hello, Anne-Marie.
Anne-Marie.   What is there in your classroom?
Pierre.   There are some tables and some chairs.
Sophie.   There are also some shelves and lots of books...
Pierre.   ... and exercise books.
Sophie.   Do you have your pencil-case, Anne-Marie?
Anne-Marie.   Yes, I have my pencil-case.
Pierre.   What do you have in your pencil-case?
Anne-Marie.   I have...a pen, three crayons, a rubber, a ruler and a calculator.
Sophie.   You have a calculator?
Anne-Marie.   Yes! Here is my calculator!
Sophie.   And you, Pierre, do you have a calculator?
Pierre.   No, but I have my father's calculator.
Sophie.   It's your father's calculator? Is he happy (about that)?
Pierre.   No!

Exercice 2.6

Où est...? = Where is ...?
Voici ... = Here is ...

e.g.   Où est mon stylo? = Where is my pen?
        Voici mon stylo. = Here is my pen.

Exercice 2.7

1.   Le livre de Pierre
2.   La trousse de Sophie
3.   La calculatrice de Chantal
4.   L'ordinateur du garçon
5.   Le sac de la fille
6.   Le professeur de l'élève
7.   L'ami du garçon
8.   L'amie des filles
9.   Un ami / Une amie du professeur
10.   Les élèves du professeur
11.   Les stylos de Bernard
12.   La règle de Nicolas
13.   Les cahiers de David
14.   La calculatrice d'Anne-Marie
15.   La salle de classe des élèves
16.   La carte du professseur
17.   Les ami(e)s de la fille
18.   La porte de la salle de classe
19.   La gomme de Pierre
20.   La chaise du professeur

Les verbes: avoir – CD:9

Avoir: Present Tense: all parts are read out.

Exercice 2.8 – CD:10

1.   Oui, il a un cahier.   Yes, he has a book.
2.   Oui elle a une gomme.   Yes, she has a rubber.

3.	Oui, nous avons des crayons.　　　　Yes we have (some) pencils.
4.	Oui, vous avez des étagères dans
	la classe.　　　　　　　　　　　　Yes, you have shelves in the classroom.
5.	Oui, ils ont un ordinateur dans
	la classe.　　　　　　　　　　　　Yes, they have a computer in the classroom.

Exercice 2.9

1.	J'**ai** un cahier.　　　　　　　　　I have an exercise book.
2.	Tu **as** un livre.　　　　　　　　　You have a book.
3.	Nous **avons** des crayons.　　　　　We have some pencils.
4.	Vous **avez** des trousses.　　　　　You (pl.) have some pencil-cases.
5.	Tu **as** les cahiers de Chantal?　　　Do you have Chantal's exercise books?
6.	Paul et Marcel **ont** les stylos de Jean.	Paul and Marcel have Jean's pens.
7.	On **a** une règle?　　　　　　　　Do we have a ruler?
8.	Elle **a** ta trousse.　　　　　　　　She has your pencil-case.
9.	Mon ami **a** une gomme.　　　　　My friend has a rubber.
10.	Oui, il **a** des cartes.　　　　　　　Yes he has some cards/maps.

Les verbes: être - CD:11

The irregular verb être in the present tense: all parts are read aloud.

La rentrée

Good morning sir. I am Nicolas.

You are in my class, Nicolas?
Yes, sir.

Is he in my class?
Yes, sir.

What about you (pl.)? You (pl.) are also in my class?
Yes sir. We are also in the class.

They (f.) are in my class?
Yes sir!

And the boys...
Yes!

He's mad, the teacher!

Exercice 2.10

1.	Je **suis** Nicolas.　　　　　　　　I am Nicolas.
2.	Il **est** dans la classe.　　　　　　He is in the class.
3.	Vous **êtes** dans ma classe?　　　　Are you in my class?
4.	Nous **sommes** dans la classe.　　　We are in the class.

5.   Les filles **sont** dans la classe.   The girls are in the class.
6.   Le prof **est** fou!   The teacher is mad!
7.   Où **est** ma règle?   Where is my ruler?
8.   Elle **est** dans ta trousse!   It is in your pencil-case!
9.   Mon stylo **est** dans mon sac?   Is my pen in my bag?
10.   Oui, il **est** dans ton sac.   Yes, it is in your bag.

Exercice 2.11 – CD:12

Charles.   Jean-Paul, do you have my geography (exercise) book, please?
Jean-Paul.   No. It is in your school-bag.
Charles.   Oh, yes. Thank you.
Delphine.   Catherine, where is your pen?
Catherine.   My red pen? It is under my pencil-case, on the desk, beside my ruler.
Frédéric.   Where are the Maths books, please, sir?
Prof.   Between the dictionary and the radio.
Frédéric.   Thank you, sir.
Prof.   Charles, where is your ball?
Charles.   It is behind my bag.
Prof.   And your bag?
Charles.   My bag is in the cupboard in front of my exercise books.
Prof.   And your homework? Where is your homework?
Charles.   Oh bother! It's in the bin!

Exercice 2.12 – CD:13

Prof.   Hello, Marc. Do you have your pencil case?
Marc.   Hello, Sir. Yes, I have my pencil case here. I also have my French textbook and my Maths exercise book.
Prof.   What do you have in your pencil case?
Marc.   I have five pencils and two pens, my ruler, my calculator and a rubber.
Prof.   You have two pens?
Marc.   Yes. I have my pen and Pierre's pen.
Prof.   Ah. Pierre's pen is red?
Marc.   Yes, sir, it is red.

1.   (a)   Marc **a** deux stylos.
    (b)   Le **prof** dit: 'Bonjour, Marc.'
    (c)   Marc répond: '**Bonjour**, Monsieur.'
    (d)   **Le** stylo de Pierre **est** rouge.
    (e)   Marc dit: «j'ai cinq **crayons et** deux **stylos**.»

2.   (a)   faux
    (b)   je ne sais pas (an opportunity to learn this phrase!)
    (c)   vrai
    (d)   faux
    (e)   faux

3. (a) Le stylo de Pierre est rouge.   Pierre's pen is red.
    (b) Marc a deux stylos dans sa trousse.   Marc has two pens in his pencil-case.
    (c) Le garçon s'appelle Marc.   The boy is called Marc.
    (d) Marc a un livre de français.   Marc has a French textbook.
    (e) Il répond: «Bonjour, Monsieur.»   He replies: 'Hello, sir.'

Exercice 2.13

1. Marc is in Pierre's classroom.
2. He has a pencil-case. In the pencil-case there are pens and pencils.
3. Sophie's ruler is in Anne-Marie's pencil-case.
4. Bernard's calculator is red.
5. The boy in the classroom is called Pierre.

Exercice 2.14

1. J'ai un an.   I am one year old.
2. J'ai trois ans.   I am three years old.
3. J'ai huit ans.   I am eight years old.
4. J'ai dix ans.   I am ten years old.
5. J'ai onze ans.   I am eleven years old.
6. J'ai douze ans / Nous avons douze ans.   I am / we are twelve years old.

Exercice 2.15

1. J'**ai** une trousse.   I have a pencil-case.
2. Tu **as** dix ans Tiffany?   Are you ten, Tiffany?
3. Monsieur Béchet **est** devant la salle.   Monsieur Béchet is in front of the class.
4. Tu **as** un stylo?   Do you have a pen?
5. Je **suis** Nicolas et j'**ai** onze ans.   I'm Nicolas and I'm eleven.
6. J'**ai** trois crayons.   I have 3 pencils.
7. Alors, Charles et moi, nous **avons** douze ans.   Well, Charles and I, we are 12.
8. Les élèves dans la salle de classe **ont** des livres.   The pupils in the classroom have books.
9. Philippe **est** un ami de Charles.   Philippe is a friend of Charles
10. Nicolas **a** une amie qui s'appelle Chantal.   Nicolas has a friend called Chantal.
11. Nous **avons** beaucoup d'amis à l'école.   We have lots of friends at school.
12. Où **sont** mes cahiers?   Where are my exercise books?
13. Vous **avez** deux gommes?   Do you have two rubbers?
14. Les étagères **sont** derrière la porte.   The shelves are behind the door.

15. Le livre de Charles **est** devant la télévision.

Charles's book is in front of the television

16. Tes crayons **sont** entre les cahiers et la radio.

Your pencils are between the exercise books and the radio.

Exercice 2.16

STYLO	GOMME	CARTE	PORTE
GARÇON	FILLE	PROFESSEUR	CALCULATRICE

Vive la France! 2

(a) The motor car industry is very important in France. The three main types are Citroën, Renault and Peugeot. Here is a Citroën 2CV of 1950. It is a famous car.

(b) En France, l'industrie automobile est **très importante**.
Citroën, Renault et Peugeot sont les **marques** principales.
La 2CV ('Deux Chevaux') est une **voiture célèbre**.

(c) la voiture (the others are people)

Chapitre 3

Chez Nous

Exercice 3.1 - CD:14

Here is Georges.
Here is Martine.
Georges is in the bathroom.
Martine is in her bedroom.

(In speech bubble:)
Georges.   Mmm, breakfast!

Maman.   Georges! Are you in the bathroom?
Georges.   No, Mum, I'm coming!
Maman.   Martine! Are you in your bedroom?
Martine.   No, Mum. I'm coming, right away! Are you eating already, Dad?
Papa.   Yes, Martine. I'm eating breakfast.

(In speech bubbles:)
Martine.   I love breakfast!
Papa.   The coffee is good.

Georges and Martine are in the kitchen. Mum is preparing breakfast. Dad is looking at the paper. Georges is eating a *tartine* with his tea and Martine is eating a *croissant* with her chocolate. They are eating breakfast. Martine likes croissants; they are delicious! Georges loves tartines; they are delicious!

Exercice 3.1

Corrections shown in italics:

1.   Georges adore *les tartines.*
2.   Martine mange *un croissant.*
3.   *Maman* prépare le petit déjeuner.
4.   *Ils* mangent dans *la cuisine.*
5.   *Papa* regarde le journal.

Les verbes du premier groupe: ER - CD:15

The verb regarder, in the present tense, is read out.

Exercice 3.2

1. arriver = to arrive

j'arrive	nous arrivons
tu arrives	vous arrivez
il arrive	ils arrivent
elle arrive	elles arrivent

2. chanter = to sing

je chante	nous chantons
tu chantes	vous chantez
il chante	ils chantent
elle chante	elles chantent

3. jouer = to play

je joue	nous jouons
tu joues	vous jouez
il joue	ils jouent
elle joue	elles jouent

4. habiter = to live

j'habite	nous habitons
tu habites	vous habitez
il habite	ils habitent
elle habite	elles habitent

5. donner = to give

je donne	nous donnons
tu donnes	vous donnez
il donne	ils donnent
elle donne	elles donnent

6. aimer = to like

j'aime	nous aimons
tu aimes	vous aimez
il aime	ils aiment
elle aime	elles aiment

7. parler = to speak

je parle	nous parlons
tu parles	vous parlez
il parle	ils parlent
elle parle	elles parlent

8. écouter = to listen to

j'écoute	nous écoutons
tu écoutes	vous écoutez
il écoute	ils écoutent
elle écoute	elles écoutent

9. manger = to eat

je mange	nous mangeons
tu manges	vous mangez
il mange	ils mangent
elle mange	elles mangent

Exercice 3.3

1. Elle jou**e** — She plays
2. Nous chant**ons** — We sing
3. Je donn**e** — I give
4. Madame arriv**e** — Madam arrives
5. J'écout**e** — I listen
6. Tu habit**es** — You live
7. Charles ador**e** — Charles loves
8. Martine mang**e** — Martine is eating
9. Nous habit**ons** — We live
10. Elles jou**ent** — They (f.) play
11. Il regard**e** — He looks
12. Vous écout**ez** — You listen
13. J'aim**e** — I like
14. Nous mang**eons** — We eat
15. Ils donn**ent** — They give

Exercice 3.4

1. J'aime
2. Tu manges
3. Il chante
4. Elle arrive
5. Nous mangeons
6. Vous adorez
7. Ils habitent
8. Elles regardent
9. On donne
10. Elle habite

Exercice 3.5

1. Non, nous écoutons.
2. Non, ils jouent.
3. Non, elle mange.
4. Non, vous écoutez le lecteur de CDs.
5. Oui! J'aime le français!

Exercice 3.6

1.   donner, manger, chanter, garder, aimer, laver, passer, tartiner, adorer, écouter

2.   donner = to give

je donne	nous donnons
tu donnes	vous donnez
il donne	ils donnent
elle donne	elles donnent

manger = to eat

je mange	nous mangeons
tu manges	vous mangez
il mange	ils mangent
elle mange	elles mangent

chanter = to sing

je chante	nous chantons
tu chantes	vous chantez
il chante	ils chantent
elle chante	elles chantent

garder = to keep

je garde	nous gardons
tu gardes	vous gardez
il garde	ils gardent
elle garde	elles gardent

aimer = to like

j'aime	nous aimons
tu aimes	vous aimez
il aime	ils aiment
elle aime	elles aiment

laver = to wash

je lave	nous lavons
tu laves	vous lavez
il lave	ils lavent
elle lave	elles lavent

passer = to pass

je passe	nous passons
tu passes	vous passez
il passe	ils passent
elle passe	elles passent

tartiner = to spread (on bread)

je tartine	nous tartinons
tu tartines	vous tartinez
il tartine	ils tartinent
elle tartine	elles tartinent

adorer = to love

j'adore	nous adorons
tu adores	vous adorez
il adore	ils adorent
elle adore	elles adorent

écouter = to listen to

j'écoute	nous écoutons
tu écoutes	vous écoutez
il écoute	ils écoutent
elle écoute	elles écoutent

Exercice 3.7 - CD:16

Mum loves singing, and she often listens to the radio. While Georges and Martine are eating tartines, Mum is listening to the radio and is singing.

'The coffee is very good' says Dad. 'Is there any more coffee?'

'Yes, dear' says Mum. 'Give (me) your bowl.'

'Thank you,' says Dad.

He gives his bowl to Mum. On the table with the coffee pot there are four bowls and some orange juice. There are plates, knives, forks, four glasses and some spoons. There are also butter and jam. Dad's bowl is blue. On Martine's bowl there is her name - Martine.

1.   She is singing.
2.   They are eating tartines.
3.   He thinks it is very good.
4.   There are four bowls, plates, knives, forks, four glasses and spoons. There are also butter and jam.
5.   Martine's name is on her bowl.

Exercice 3.8

Pupils choose their own breakfast from the 8,00€ menu. Two items, with a choice of drink, is acceptable.

e.g.   Un croissant, un pain au chocolat et un jus d'orange, s'il vous plaît.

Exercice 3.9

1. Voici sa maison.
2. Voilà sa maison.
3. Où est ta maison?
4. J'aime ses parents.
5. Il y a un livre dans son sac.
6. Il y a un chien dans sa maison.
7. Il y a douze élèves dans sa classe.
8. Voilà mes parents!
9. Voici son chat.
10. Voici mon amie: elle est dans ma classe.

Exercice 3.10 – CD:17

Peter, an English friend, arrives at Martine's and Georges' house.

Martine.   Hello Peter!
Peter.   Hello!
Martine.   Shall we have a look round the house?
Peter.   Yes.
Martine.   Right. Here, we're in the entrance hall. On the ground floor we have three rooms. In front of us, there's the kitchen. On the left, there's the sitting room and on the right, the dining room. Upstairs, there are four bedrooms. Shall we go up?
Peter.   Yes. But where's the bathroom?
Martine.   Here's the bathroom, between my bedroom and my parents' bedroom.

Matching the numbers to the rooms on the plan:

1. le salon
2. la cuisine
3. la salle à manger
4. l'entrée (given)
5. la chambre des parents
6. la salle de bains
7. la chambre de Martine (given)
8. et 9. des chambres.

Exercice 3.11

1 + d	Martine arrive et **mange le petit déjeuner**.
2 + a	Dans la maison **il y a un chien et un chat**.
3 + b	Voici une photo **de mes parents**.
4 + e	Le cahier de Sophie **est sur la table**.
5 + c	Il y a trois livres **et douze crayons**.

Exercice 3.12

1. Paul **mange** le petit déjeuner.
   Paul eats breakfast.
2. Maman et Charles **arrivent** dans la salle à manger.
   Mum and Charles arrive in the dining room.
3. Sophie **est** dans la salle de bains.
   Sophie is in the bathroom.
4. Paul et Georges **regardent** la télévision.
   Paul and Georges are watching television.
5. Marie-Claire, tu **écoutes** la radio?
   Marie-Claire, are you listening to the radio?

Exercice 3.13

1. + (c)   la cuisine = the kitchen
2. + (d)   la salle de bains = the bathroom
3. + (a)   la salle à manger = the dining room
4. + (b)   la salle de classe = the classroom

Exercice 3.14

Pupils are asked to make a crossword using the words given. An example is given below:

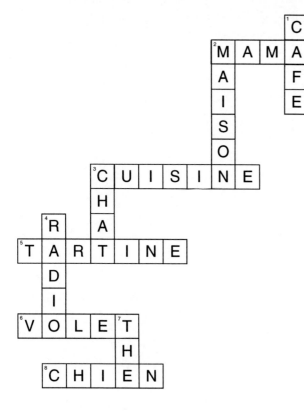

Horizontalement
2. She's obviously not your father.
3. A style of cooking in this room.
5. Yummy with chocolate spread.
6. Shut that please!
8. Woof, woof!

Verticalement
1. A hot drink in a fast-food restaurant?
2. House.
3. Not always a friend of 8.
4. Tune it in to listen.
7. Time for a cupper?

Exercice 3.15

a. **Nous** regardons la télévision.
b. **Tu** écoutes la radio?
c. **Ils / Elles** chantent à la chapelle.
d. **Vous** adorez les croissants, n'est-ce pas?
e. **Je** m'appelle Monsieur Banane.

Vive la France! 3

(a) In France a lot of bread is eaten. At the bakery there are all sorts of bread: baguettes, round loaves, 'French' sticks, country loaves... There are also croissants! Mmm, delicious!

(b) BOULANGERIE, BAGUETTE, DÉLICIEUX, CROISSANT

(c) Faux, faux, faux.

(d) En France on mange le pain dans la cuisine ou dans la salle **à manger**.
     À la boulangerie, il y a toutes sortes de **pain**.
     Maman écoute **la radio** et mange **un croissant.**

Chapitre 4

La Routine - CD:18

Georges wakes up at seven o'clock.

Martine gets up at quarter past seven.

Martine gets dressed at twenty past seven.

Georges washes at half past seven.

Martine and Georges come down at quarter to eight.

It is eight o'clock. It is breakfast time.

Les verbes pronominaux - CD:19

The reflexive verb se laver, in the present tense, is read out.

Exercice 4.1

1. She gets up.
2. I wash myself.
3. You (pl.) wake up.
4. We get dressed.
5. You (sing.) wake up.
6. They (m.) wake up.
7. We get up.
8. You (sing.) wash yourself.
9. They (f.) get up.
10. You (pl.) wash yourselves.

Exercice 4.2

1. Elle se réveille.
2. Tu t'habilles.
3. Je me lave.
4. Vous vous lavez.
5. Tu te réveilles.
6. Martine se lave.
7. Elle se lève.
8. Nous nous réveillons.
9. Ils se réveillent.
10. Il s'habille.

Quelle heure est-il? - CD:20

Exercice 4.3

1. (a) huit heures trente / huit heures et demie
   (b) cinq heures moins dix
   (c) trois heures et quart
   (d) neuf heures et demie
   (e) midi
   (f) minuit
   (g) sept heures quinze / sept heures et quart
   (h) cinq heures quarante-cinq / six heures moins le quart

2.   (a)   dix heures du soir
       (b)   trois heures de l'après-midi
       (c)   dix heures et demie du matin
       (d)   deux heures dix de l'après-midi
       (e)   six heures et quart du soir.
       (f)   sept heures vingt du matin
       (g)   cinq heures et quart du matin
       (h)   sept heures vingt-cinq du soir

3   (a)   Il est cinq heures moins le quart.
      (b)   Il est sept heures moins le quart.
      (c)   Il est sept heures.
      (d)   Il est huit heures et demie.
      (e)   Il est neuf heures.
      (f)   Il est dix heures moins le quart.

Exercice 4.4 – CD:21

Martine.   Hi, Dad!
Papa.   Hello, Martine. Hello, Georges!
Georges.   Hello, Dad! Hello, Mum! How are you?
Maman.   Fine, my dear. What time is it, please?
Georges.   I do not know.
Maman.   Martine, what time is it?
Martine.   It is... five past eight.
Papa.   Five past eight? Well then, goodbye!
Maman.   You're not eating your *tartine*?
Papa.   Oh, no! I am late!

Exercice 4.5

1.   (a)   Je me lève à ...
       (b)   Je mange le petit déjeuner à ...
       (c)   J'arrive à l'école à ...
       (d)   Je mange le déjeuner à ...
       (e)   Je quitte l'école à ...

2   (a)   Improbable   It would mean having lunch at 7.30.
      (b)   Improbable   It would mean arriving at school at lunchtime.
      (c)   Probable   8.00 pm is normal for watching a film on tv.
      (d)   Improbable   Sophie wouldn't leave the house at 3.00 am.
      (e)   Probable   Having Maths at 9.00 is quite normal.

Les verbes: faire - CD:22

The irregular verb faire, in the present tense, is read out.

Exercice 4.6 – CD:23

Paul.   Well, then, Jacques. What do you do at home?
Jacques.   At home?
Paul.   Yes, to help your parents?
Jacques.   Right, today, I tidy my bedroom, I make my bed, I do the housework and I do the washing up.
Paul.   Every day?
Jacques.   Yes, every day! Well... sometimes. Well... no!

1.   Jacques tidies his room, makes his bed, does the housework, and does the washing up.
2.   He doesn't do them every day!

Exercice 4.7

1.   I do my homework at 7 o'clock in the evening.
2.   We do some shopping every day.
3.   Dad does the washing up after breakfast.
4.   You go skiing in the Alps.
5.   They go for a walk after lunch.

Exercice 4.8

1.   Philippe **fait** du cheval dans la forêt.
      Philippe goes horse-riding in the forest.
2.   Moi, je **fais** du ski à Val d'Isère.
      Me, I go skiing in Val d'Isère.
3.   Papa et Georges **font** la cuisine - quelquefois!
      Dad and Georges do the cooking - sometimes!
4.   Elle **fait** ses devoirs à cinq heures.
      She does her homework at five o'clock.
5.   Nous **faisons** des courses aujourd'hui.
      We are going shopping today.

Exercice 4.9

1.   Il fait son lit à 7 h 30.
2.   Il fait le ménage à 11 heures.
3.   Elle fait la vaisselle tous les jours.
4.   Ils font la vaisselle à 14 h 30.
5.   Tu fais la cuisine aujourd'hui.
6.   Elle fait ses devoirs à 19 heures.
7.   Ma maman fait la cuisine tous les jours.
8.   Il fait les courses à midi.
9.   Quelquefois, on fait une promenade à midi.
10.   Maman fait du cheval à 16 heures.
11.   Elles font une promenade à 17 heures.
12.   Nous faisons du ski dans les Alpes.

Les verbes: mettre - CD:24

The irregular verb mettre, in the present tense, is read out.

Exercice 4.10

1.   Nous **mettons** les crayons de Pierre dans sa trousse.
       We are putting Pierre's pencils in his pencil-case.
2.   Je **mets** mon pullover.
       I am putting on my pullover.
3.   Ils **mettent** les cahiers sur la table.
       They put their exercise books on the table.
4.   Maman **met** la table pour le petit déjeuner.
       Mum lays the table for breakfast.
5.   Vous **mettez** le café dans le bol.
       You put the coffee in the bowl.
6.   Il **met** mon cartable dans la salle de classe.
       He puts my school bag in the classroom.
7.   Elle **met** un poster dans ta chambre?
       Does she put a poster in your bedroom?
8.   Tu **mets** la table?
       Are you laying the table?

Les verbes: sortir - CD:25

The irregular verb sortir, in the present tense, is read out.

Exercice 4.11

1.   Je **sors** avec mes amis à 20 h.
       I go out with my friends at 8.00 p.m.
2.   D'habitude, c'est maman qui **sort** le chien.
       Usually it is Mum who puts the dog out.
3.   Paul! Tu **sors** les poubelles, s'il te plaît!
       Paul! Put the bins out, please!
4.   Les enfants **sortent** après le déjeuner.
       The children go out after lunch.

Exercice 4.12

Pupils are asked to say or write down the things they do to help at home, using the list of expressions and vocabulary on page 43. Between three and five should be acceptable.

There is a series of four cartoon pictures to accompany this.
(In speech bubbles:)
Nicolas.   Who does the cooking in your house?
Georges.   Usually, it is Mum...but sometimes it is Dad. My sister sometimes puts the bins out... but she does not walk the dog.

La négation - CD:26

Examples of the sound of sentences in thc negative are given.

Exercice 4.13 - CD:27

Patrick.   What do you do in the evenings at home?
Cédric.   Me? It depends. Usually I watch tv in my bedroom before dinner.
Patrick.   Don't you do your homework?
Cédric.   Yes! I do my homework after dinner. What about you?
Patrick.   Not me.
Maman.   Patrick doesn't do his homework after dinner. He doesn't listen to the radio, he doesn't watch TV. He is tired in the evening.

1.   He usually watches television in his bedroom before dinner.
2.   He does not do his homework because he is tired.

Exercice 4.14

1.   Patrick ne fait pas ses devoirs.   Patrick does not do his homework.
2.   Mélanie ne passe pas l'aspirateur.   Mélanie does not do the hoovering.
3.   Linda ne fait pas la vaisselle.   Linda does not do the washing up.
4.   Elles ne sortent pas les poubelles.   They (f.) do not put the bins out.
5.   Maman ne met pas toujours la table.   Mum does not always lay the table.

Exercice 4.15

1.   Georges et papa font la vaisselle.   Georges and Dad do the washing up.
2.   La sœur de Paul promène les chiens.   Paul's sister walks the dogs.
3.   D'habitude je regarde la télé le soir.   Usually I watch tv in the evenings.
4.   Martine écoute la radio.   Martine listens to the radio.
5.   Elle aime les croissants.   She likes croissants.

Exercice 4.16

1.   D'habitude, je ne fais pas mes devoirs à l'école.
    Usually, I don't do my prep at school.
2.   Mon père ne regarde pas la télévision le soir.
    My father does not watch television in the evenings.
3.   Claude et Françoise ne descendent pas avant dix heures.
    Claude and Françoise don't come downstairs before 10.00.
4.   Paul, tu n'aimes pas ton café ?
    Paul, don't you like your coffee ?
5.   Je n'écoute pas la radio de 8h à 10h.
    I do not listen to the radio from 8.00 until 10.00.

Exercice 4.17

1.   Nous ne mangeons **pas de** tomates.
2.   Tu n'as **pas d'**animaux à la maison?

3. Je n'ai **pas de** devoirs.
4. Elle n'a **pas de** cahier.
5. Ils n'ont **pas de** carte dans la salle de classe.

Exercice 4.18

1. Philippe a des crayons, mais il n'a pas de stylos.
2. J'ai des assiettes, mais je n'ai pas de verres.
3. Nous avons un couteau, mais nous n'avons pas de fourchettes.
4. Papa a du café, mais il n'a pas de jus d'orange.
5. Nicolas ne regarde pas la télévision. Il fait ses devoirs.
6. Maman ne mange pas de croissants aujourd'hui.

Vive la France! 4

(a) Travelling in France is not difficult: the trains are fast and comfortable. The government encourages people to travel by train: for long journeys there is the high speed train; but there are also lots of little trains that are slower (less fast).

(b) Missing words:

Les voyages en France ne sont pas **difficiles**.
Le TGV est **rapide** et **confortable**.
Le TGV est pour les **grandes** distances.
Le gouvernement **encourage** la population à voyager par le train.

Les **trains** sont très rapides!
Les trains sont **rapides** et confortables.
Il y **a** beaucoup de petits trains.
Pour les grandes distances **il** y a le TGV.
Les voyages **ne** sont pas difficiles.

(<u>T</u>GV, <u>r</u>apides, <u>a</u>ussi, <u>il</u> y a, <u>ne</u> : TRAIN)

Chapitre 5

On va à l'école! – Les verbes: aller – CD:28

The irregular verb aller, in the present tense, is read out.

Exercice 5.1

1.	Marc va à l'école en voiture.	Marc goes to school by car.
2.	Nous allons à Paris par le train.	We go to Paris by train.
3.	Tu vas à Nice en car.	You go by coach to Nice
4.	Je vais chez moi à pied.	I go home on foot.
5.	Ils vont à Calais en bateau.	They go to Calais by boat.
6.	Vous allez à l'école à vélo.	You go to school by bicycle.

Les jours de la semaine - CD:29

The days of the week in French are read out.

Exercice 5.2 – CD:30

It is Tuesday morning. Marie-Claire and Paul arrive at school by bike. Marie-Claire's and Paul's friends are chatting in the classroom. Marie-Claire likes Tuesdays; it is her favourite day. Why? Because she has two hours of Natural Sciences, and she adores Science. After break, she has an hour of English. She likes speaking English a lot.

Paul does not much like Tuesdays. He does not like working. He loves sport, but he has no sport on Tuesdays. He has an hour of French and an hour of German - and he hates languages! But he likes History-Geog.; it is his favourite subject.

1.   (a)   C'est **lundi** matin.
   It is Monday morning.
   (b)   Marie-Claire et Paul vont à l'école **à vélo**.
   Marie-Claire and Paul go to school by bike.
   (c)   La matière préférée de Marie-Claire, c'est **les sciences**.
   Marie-Claire's favourite subject is Science.
   (d)   La matière préférée de Paul, c'est **l'histoire-géo**.
   Paul's favourite subject is History-Geog.
   (e)   **Marie-Claire** aime les mardis à l'école. **Paul** n'aime pas les mardis.
   Marie-Claire likes Tuesdays at school. Paul does not like Tuesdays.

2.   (a)   Paul et sa sœur Marie-Claire aim**ent** le collège.
   Paul and his sister Marie-Claire like school.
   (b)   Paul détest**e** l'allemand.
   Paul hates German.
   (c)   Les amis discut**ent** dans la cour pendant la pause.
   The friends chat in the playground during break.

(d) Nous parl**ons** beaucoup avant les classes.
We talk a lot before lessons.

(e) J'ador**e** les lundis.
I love Mondays.

3. Pupils should write out their timetable in French, by hand or on a computer, using the French names for days of the week and lessons (p.50).

4. Pupils should write a paragraph on days they themselves like and don't like, using the paragraph on page 51 as an example.

Exercice 5.3 – CD:31

Jean-Pierre. Hi, Paul!
Paul. Hi! What time is it?
Jean-Pierre. Twenty past eight.
Paul. Oh no! I've got English in ten minutes. And you, do you have English today?
Jean-Pierre. No, but I have an hour of music. I love music.
Marie-Claire. Hang on! Hello, Anne!
Anne. Hello! Is it ... Tuesday today?
Marie-Claire. Yes. It's Tuesday.
Anne. Cool! I love Tuesdays.
Marie-Claire. Why?
Anne. Because I have Natural Sciences. I love bio(logy)!
Marie-Claire. You like Biology? Not me.

Exercice 5.4 – CD:32

A. The following adjectives change their sound in the feminine:

grande, petite, anglaise, intelligente, intéressante, française, bavarde, méchante.

Voici les adjectifs:

(a)	grande	(i)	intelligente
(b)	petite	(j)	intéressante
(c)	anglaise	(k)	française
(d)	amusante	(l)	bavarde
(e)	fatiguée	(m)	méchante
(f)	chouette	(n)	bête
(g)	sage	(o)	timide
(h)	sévère	(p)	jeune

B. Each phrase must include one example each of an adjective in the masculine form and one in the feminine.

De quelle couleur? - CD:33

The following colours change their sound in the feminine:

au masculin		au féminin
blanc	>	blan**che**
brun	>	bru**ne**
gris	>	gris**e**
vert	>	ver**te**
violet	>	viole**tte**

Exercice 5.5

C'est un vélo rose.
C'est un livre bleu.
C'est une voiture verte.
C'est un tableau blanc.
C'est une voiture rouge.

Exercice 5.6

Pupils must design a poster that could be put up on a classroom wall for younger children to learn the French colours.

Exercice 5.7 – CD:34

Claire. Sophie, do you have art today?
Sophie.   Yes. After the 11 o'clock break.
Claire. Do you like the new art teacher?
Sophie.   Oh, yes! He is really nice.
Claire. That's true. Unfortunately, I don't have art on Thursdays. I have Latin after break. I find Latin difficult. I am useless (at it)!
Laurent.   Cédric, do you find Latin difficult?
Cédric.   No, not really. But then I am quite good at languages.
Laurent.   Me, I am not much good at Latin. I prefer craft.
Cédric.   It's the same for me. I like that too.

Exercice 5.8

1.   Pupils should read the French version of the following passage then re-write it, changing the details in bold to suit themselves in 'real life':

   My name is **Eric**. I am **thirteen** years old. I go to school in **Niort in France**. My school is called the **École St. Agnan**. I like school a lot, because **I have many friends**. I eat **in the dining room**. In the dining room the food is **good**! My favourite subject is **ICT**. But I also like **Latin and English**. I am good at **Maths**; I find that the teacher is very **strict**. I love **sport**, but I am **useless** at it.

2.   LATIN   ANGLAIS   HISTOIRE   MATHS   ESPAGNOL

3.   (a)   vrai
     (b)   vrai
     (c)   faux
     (d)   faux
     (e)   faux

Exercice 5.9

1. Claire est grande mais elle est méchante.
   Claire is tall but she is naughty.
2. Cédric n'est pas fort en maths.
   Cédric is not good at Maths.
3. Nathalie a une amie bavarde qui s'appelle Anne.
   Nathalie has a talkative friend called Anne.
4. Marie lit un livre intéressant.
   Marie is reading an interesting book.
5. La maison est blanche et noire.
   The house is white and black.
6. Cédric trouve le latin facile.
   Cédric finds Latin easy.
7. Anne n'est pas très intelligente.
   Anne isn't very intelligent.
8. Ma matière préférée, c'est la géographie.
   My favourite subject is Geography.
9. La prof de dessin, Madame Schmidt, a une voiture bleue.
   The art teacher, Mrs Schmidt, has a blue car.
10. Mon amie Aurélie est absente.
    My friend Aurélie is absent.

Exercice 5.10

1. Tu n'**écoutes** pas!
   You are not listening!
2. Mais ce n'**est** pas intéressant!
   But it isn't interesting!
3. Claire, tu **as** un stylo?
   Claire, do you have a pen?
4. Oui. J'**ai** trois stylos et un crayon dans ma trousse.
   Yes. I have three pens and a pencil in my pencil-case.
5. Si nous **parlons** en classe, le prof n'**est** pas content.
   If we talk in class, the teacher is not happy.
6. Henri et Jules **habitent** à trois kilomètres de Niort.
   Henri and Jules live three kilometres from Niort.
7. Charlotte **aime** chanter avec ses amies.
   Charlotte likes singing with her girlfriends.
8. Elles **chantent** tous les dimanches à la chapelle.
   They (f.) sing every Sunday in the chapel.
9. Vous **allez** à Niort en voiture?
   Are you going to Niort by car?
10. Oui. Nous **donnons** un cadeau à ton cousin.
    Yes. We are giving a present to your cousin.

Les adjectifs (suite) – CD:35

Pupils should listen carefully to the adjectives in their masculine and feminine forms.

Exercice 5.11

Across
2. beau
5. intéressante
6. vieux

Down
1. paresseuse
3. fort
4. belle

Exercice 5.12

1. Un élève qui ne travaille pas beaucoup est **paresseux.**
2. Quelque chose qui n'est pas difficile est **facile.**
3. Une grand-mère qui n'est pas jeune est **vieille.**
4. J'adore les maths – c'est ma matière **préférée.**
5. Une visite qui n'est pas désagréable est **agréable.**
6. Une fille qui parle beaucoup est **bavarde.**
7. Un élève qui n'est pas faible en français est **fort.**
8. Quelque chose que j'adore manger est **délicieux.**
9. Un professeur qui n'est pas stupide est **intelligent.**
10. Un garçon qui n'est pas petit est **grand.**

Exercice 5.13

1. Les garçons sont paresseux.*
2. Les filles sont heureuses.*
3. Les trains sont (-ils) dangereux?*
4. Le professeur est nouveau.
5. Ma trousse est nouvelle / neuve.
6. Voici mon premier cahier. Il est rouge.
7. Mon père est beau et ma mère est belle.
8. Mon prof de français est très sympa.
9. Ma grand-mère est très vieille.
10. Le tableau dans la salle de classe est blanc.

* The plural forms of adjectives are covered on p.76 of the pupil's book. In subsequent print runs, questions 1-3 will be amended as follows:

1.	The boy is lazy.	Le garçon est paresseux
2.	The girl is happy.	La fille est heureuse
3.	Is the train dangerous?	Le train est(-il) dangereux?

Vive la France! 5

(a)   In France the teacher stays in the classroom. At break, there is a different person who accompanies the pupils (the boys and girls). It is a *surveillant(e)*. In France, the teachers work in the classroom, and the *surveillants* accompany the pupils to/in the school dining room and (when they go) outside.

(b)   En France les professeurs ne sont pas avec les enfants à la pause. Les professeurs sont en classe. Les professeurs n'accompagnent pas les élèves à la cantine.

Chapitre 6

La date, les numéros, les prix
Mon anniversaire CD:36

The numbers from 1 to 31 and the months are read out in French.

Exercice 6.1 – CD:37

Claire.   What day is it today, Dad?
Papa.   It's Saturday.
Claire.   It's Saturday? It's the weekend!
Philippe.   When is Mum's birthday?
Papa.   It's the 28th February. It's today!
Claire.   What are we buying?
Philippe.   She loves chocolate.
Papa.   Chocolate? That's not interesting.
Philippe.   Me, I don't have much money!

Philippe and Claire go to Belleville with Dad. They go by car, for Belleville is three kilometres away from home. They are looking for presents for Mum's birthday. Her birthday is on the 28th February. They go into Monsieur Meunier's shop, the jewellers. They look at a bracelet and some silver earrings.

Claire.   This bracelet is superb!
Papa.   Excuse me, sir, how much is this bracelet, please?
Jeweller.   This bracelet here? 55 euros, sir.
Philippe.   Cor! It's too expensive!
Papa.   Me, I am going to buy the bracelet.
Jeweller.   Right then, 55 euros please.
Papa.   Here you are.
Jeweller.   Thank you, sir. Goodbye.
Papa.   Good bye, sir. Right, children. Where are we going now?
Claire.   We must buy (literally: it is necessary to buy) a birthday card for Mum!
Philippe.   They are expensive, cards!

1.   It is on Saturday.
2.   He's planning to buy chocolate.
3.   He thinks it is not interesting.
4.   They go to the jeweller's, Monsieur Meunier. They look at bracelets and earrings, and decide to buy a nice bracelet for 55 euros.
5.   Claire suggests they go to buy Mum a card. Philippe says that cards are expensive.

Exercice 6.2

1. 4
2. 24
3. 34
4. 39
5. 41

6. 46
7. 55
8. 73
9. 83
10. 93

Exercice 6.3

1. quarante-quatre
2. trente-et-un
3. dix-sept
4. trente-neuf
5. cinquante-cinq

6. soixante-quatre
7. soixante-quinze
8. quatre-vingt-huit
9. quatre-vingt-dix
10. quatre-vingt-quatorze

Les numéros de téléphone - CD:38

The telephone numbers are read aloud in groups of two digits:

(a) zéro deux, cinquante et un, quatre-vingt-dix, cinquante-cinq, zéro cinq
(b) zéro trois, quarante-neuf, quatre-vingt-cinq, quatre-vingt-sept, quatre-vingt-neuf
(c) zéro six, soixante-seize, soixante-douze, vingt-trois, quinze
(d) zéro quatre, trente-trois, soixante-six, soixante-neuf, soixante-dix-neuf

Les verbes: acheter - CD:39

The slightly irregular –er verb acheter, in the present tense, is read aloud.

Exercice 6.4

1. 2 kilos d'oranges coûtent **3,00€**.
2. 4 melons coûtent **10,00€**.
3. 3 kilos de tomates coûtent **4,50€**.
4. Les carottes coûtent **0,85€** le kilo.
5. Les pommes de terre coûtent **1,75€** le kilo.
6. Les **tomates** et les **oranges** coûtent 1,50€ le kilo.

Exercice 6.5

1. Nous **achetons** 2 kilos de carottes.
2. J'**achète** des pommes de terre et un melon.
3. Elle **achète** cinq melons.
4. Ils **achètent** des tomates et des pommes.
5. Vous **achetez** des oranges?
6. Tu **achètes** des pommes pour moi, s'il te plaît.

Deux verbes irréguliers:

Vouloir – CD:40

The verb vouloir, in the present tense, is read aloud.

Pouvoir – CD:41

The verb pouvoir, in the present tense, is read aloud.

Exercice 6.6

1.	Tu **veux** regarder la télé?	Do you want to watch tv?
2.	Je **veux** écouter la radio.	I want to listen to the radio.
3.	Nous **voulons** manger tout de suite.	We want to eat straight away.
4.	Elles **veulent** acheter des cadeaux.	They want to buy some presents.
5.	Vous **voulez** aller en ville?	Do you want to go into town?

Exercice 6.7

1. Tu peux manger à 19 h.
2. Nous pouvons regarder le film.
3. Elle peut rester chez moi / à ma maison.
4. Je peux aller à l'école par le train.
5. Ils peuvent acheter des pommes au marché.

Exercice 6.8

1. Linda **veut** acheter une carte por son ami.
   Linda wants to buy a card for her friend.
2. Elle ne **peut** pas, parce qu'elle n'**a** pas d'argent.
   She can't, because she does not have any money.
3. Philippe et Claire **veulent** chercher un cadeau.
   Philippe and Claire want to look for a present.
4. Ils ne **peuvent** pas trouver le cadeau qu'ils **veulent**.
   They can't find the present that they want.
5. Tu **veux** aller à la piscine?
   Do you want to go to the swimming pool?
6. Oui, je **veux** bien, mais je ne **peux** pas.
   Yes, I do, but I can't.

Exercice 6.9 – CD:42

They enter the newsagent's shop.

Philippe. I want to look for a card for Mum.
Claire. There are only newspapers and magazines here.
Philippe. Hello, sir. I am looking for a birthday card, please.
Shopkeeper. Very sorry, young man. I do not have any birthday cards. You must go to the stationers, opposite.
Philippe. Thank you, sir.

They go to the stationery shop.

Claire.   There we are! We have a good choice of cards here. You can find a beautiful
             card for Mum.
Philippe.   Yes, that's right. Ah! Here is a beautiful card! But it is expensive. Can you
             lend me 3 euros, please?
Claire.   No! I want to keep all my money to go to the cinema on Saturday with Aurélie.

1.   He wants to buy a card for his mother.
2.   No. Claire needs all her money to go to the cinema with her friend Aurélie.

Exercice 6.10 – CD:43

Philippe **veut** acheter une carte d'anniversaire pour sa **maman**. Mais il ne **peut** pas
parce qu'il n'a pas assez d'argent. Il demande à sa soeur s'il peut emprunter trois
euros, mais Claire ne peut pas donner les trois euros à son **frère**. Elle **veut** garder
tout son argent pour aller au **cinéma** avec son amie **Aurélie**.

Philippe wants to buy a card for his Mum's birthday. But he can't, because he doesn't
have enough money. He asks his sister if he can borrow three euros, but Claire cannot give
the three euros to her brother. She wants to keep all her money to go to the cinema with
her friend Aurélie.

Exercice 6.11

1.
douze	deux	onze	un	neuf
trois	treize	vingt-trois	dix-neuf	dix
six	seize	trente-six	sept	dix-sept

2. (a)   10,40€
    (b)   32,00€
    (c)   7,17€
    (d)   93,99€
    (e)   200,25€

Exercice 6.12

Au marché

Pupils are invited to use the picture of items at a market in a memory test in French.
Teachers may wish to ensure that they are familiar with the French words first:

bananas	= des bananes	birthday card	= une carte d'anniversaire
carrots	= des carottes	pencils	= des crayons
tomatoes	= des tomates	T-shirt	= un t-shirt
books	= des livres	jeans	= un jean
melon	= un melon	sweets	= des bonbons
apples	= des pommes	shoes	= des chaussettes

Vive la France! 6

(a) There is a market in all the towns and in many villages in France. At the market one can find all sorts of products: fruit and vegetables, clothes, books, and many other things. Markets are very popular, for the French and for the tourists.

(b) des surveillants, des professeurs: you cannot buy people at the market.

(c) TOMATES
ACHETER
LIVRES
MARCHÉ
VILLAGE

Chapitre 7

Tu es comment?
Exercice 7.1 – CD:44

Anne-Marie wants a pen-friend. She finds a pen-friend in Switzerland. Her Swiss pen-friend is called Joselle Meuli. Joselle lives in Geneva, where they speak French. Here is Anne-Marie's letter:

La Roche-sur-Yon, 8th May

Dear Joselle,

Hello! You want to be my new pen-friend? Good! I am happy. I like Switzerland, especially Lake Geneva at Geneva. I am 12 years old and I have lived in La Roche-sur-Yon for 8 years.

I have long, brown hair and blue eyes. I am quite tall (I am 1 m 53 cm) and I am sporty. I also like music. My friends say that I am cheerful and optimistic.

There we are! And what about you? What are you like? Write to me soon!

Best wishes,

Anne-Marie Benoît

1. She wants to introduce herself to a new penfriend.
2. She is 12. She has long, brown hair and blue eyes. She is quite tall, sporty, cheerful and positive.
3. She asks Joselle to write a similar letter to this one, describing herself, soon.

Exercice 7.2
Dialogue 1 – CD:45

Philippe.   Cédric! Have you seen the newcomer?
Cédric.   No. What's he like?
Philippe.   He's quite well-built, not very tall but strong.
Cédric.   A little like Léon?
Philippe.   Yes. And very sporty. He goes skiing!
Cédric.   Really! How old is he?
Philippe.   14, I think.

Dialogue 2 – CD:46

Anne-Marie.   Well, Hi, Claire!
Claire.   Hi! I have a letter from my new pen-friend!
Anne-Marie.   Oh, good! Where does she live?

Claire.   In Germany.
Anne-Marie.   And what is she like?
Claire.   She is blonde, very tall, sporty. She goes riding in the Black Forest!
Anne-Marie.   Cool!

Exercice 7.3

The drawings need to represent the descriptions:

1.   He is very short. He has red frizzy hair. He is 3 years old.
2.   She is quite chubby. She has green hair and black eyes!
3.   Bobby has long red hair. He is 16 years old. He is tall and slim.

Exercice 7.4

le t-shirt est rouge;   le short est orange;
le jean est bleu;   le pull est vert;
le pantalon est gris;   la jupe est verte;
la robe est rose;   la chemise est bleue;
le chapeau est jaune;   les lunettes sont brunes;
les chaussures sont noires;   les baskets sont rouges et blancs.

Exercice 7.5 – CD:47

Sara and Nathalie go into a fashion shop, which is one kilometre from Nathalie's home, in the town centre. Nathalie has a friend, Véronique, who works in the shop on Saturdays and during the holidays. Véronique's father is the owner of the shop. Véronique is 14 years old. Nathalie is 13 years old but her birthday is in three days' time. Her friend is of medium build. She has red, curly hair and green eyes. The two friends love to dress in fashionable clothes!

Nathalie is saving up: every Sunday she puts a little money aside to buy clothes. Now she has 25 euros and can buy a dress which she can wear on her birthday.

1.   qui se trouve à un kilomètre de...
2.   au centre-ville
3.   qui travaille à la boutique
4.   pendant les vacances
5.   le samedi

Exercice 7.6

1.   Marc n'<u>aime</u> pas aller aux magasins.
      Marc doesn't like going to the shops.
2.   Marc et Claude <u>discutent</u> de la musique.
      Marc and Claude are chatting about music.
3.   Le samedi, Véronique <u>va</u> en ville.
      On Saturdays, Véronique goes into town.
4.   Ses parents <u>sont</u> propriétaires d'une boutique.
      Her parents are the owners of a shop.
5.   Nathalie ne <u>peut</u> pas acheter une robe.
      Nathalie cannot buy a dress.

Exercice 7.7

1 + (c)   Nathalie travaille *au centre-ville le samedi.*
           Nathalie works in the town centre on Saturdays
2 + (e)   Tu veux aller *au cinéma ce soir?*
           Do you want to go to the cinema this evening?
3 + (d)   Après le petit déjeuner, *je vais à la boutique.*
           After breakfast, I go to the shop.
4 + (b)   Claude achète quatre *billets d'entrée.*
           Claude buys four entrance tickets.
5 + (a)   Sara et Marc mangent *les croissants de maman.*
           Sara and Marc eat Mum's croissants.

Exercice 7.8

Pupils describe the drawings of people: hair – its length and colour, whether it is straight or curly; and the colour of each clothing item where possible. Here are some examples of descriptions:

Marie-Claire a les cheveux bruns et les yeux noirs. Elle porte un t-shirt violet et un pantalon rouge.

Sylvie a les cheveux blonds et les yeux bleus. Elle porte un t-shirt rose et un jean bleu.

Guy a les cheveux roux et les yeux verts. Il porte un pantalon bleu et un pull vert.

Caroline a les cheveux noirs et raides. Elle porte un t-shirt bleu et un short beige.

Jean-Michel porte des lunettes. Il a les cheveux noirs et courts, et il porte un pull noir et un pantalon beige.

The exercise is completed by writing a description of oneself. The letter from Anne-Marie to Joselle is a good model.

Exercice 7.9 – CD:48

During the holidays, Natalie likes to go skating. She likes to go to the skating rink with her friends Marc, Claude and Sara. Today she is wearing her black jeans and her green top. She is also wearing a black scarf. Marc is wearing dark blue trousers and a blue pullover.

'Do you like my new top?' says Natalie to Sara.

'Yes! It goes well with your jeans,' replies Sara.

Marc and Claude buy the skating rink entrance tickets. The four friends go to the counter to hire some skates.

Employee.   Yes, hello! How many of you are there?
Marc.   There are four of us.
Employee.   And what size shoe do you take?
Claude.   Me, I'm ... 42.
Marc.   Me, I take 43. But the girls, I don't know ...
Natalie.   Me, I take 36 and so does Sara.
Employee.   Good. 42, 43 and two 36. That makes ... 8 euros, please.

1. She is wearing black jeans, a green top and a black scarf.
2. Marc is wearing dark blue trousers and a blue pullover.
3. She asks Sara if she likes it.
4. She says it goes well with her jeans.
5. He asks: 'How many of you are there?'

Exercice 7.10 – CD:49

Nathalie and Sara are (lit. find themselves) in front of Véronique's shop:

Nathalie. Oh! Look at this pretty red dress! But it costs 45 euros!
Sara. Yes, it is beautiful, but it is expensive. How much money do you have?
Nathalie. Twenty-five euros. Wait! There's Véronique!
Sara. Nathalie wants to buy this dress, but it is too expensive.
Véronique. No problem! The sales start today!
Nathalie. Ah! The sales! Super!
Véronique. I (shall) ask Dad the price of this dress with the reduction!
Nathalie. Okay, then.

...

Véronique. He says that it is 30 euros ...
Nathalie. Cor ...!
Véronique. But for you, he will do (lit. he does) a special price. You can have the dress for 25 euros!
Nathalie. Cool! Thank you very much, Véronique!

1. Devant (Au dehors de) la boutique
2. Elle* coûte
3. Combien d'argent?
4. Pas de problème!
5. Les soldes
6. La réduction
7. D'accord
8. Chouette!

* 'It costs...' can also be il coûte... because *it* can be il or elle.

Exercice 7.11

PULL	SHORT	T-SHIRT	JUPE
JEAN	CHEMISE	ROBE	CHAUSSURES

Exercice 7.12

Drawings should represent the following:

1. She is tall and she has long, black hair. She is wearing a purple dress, a blue jacket and a red hat.
2. He is small and fat. He has short, frizzy hair. He wears old trousers and green trainers.
3. My friend Philippe has short, blonde hair, a tanned face, and he is 1 m 75 cm tall. He is slim, sporty and he wears cool clothes!

Vive la France! 7

(a)   French is spoken in France – of course! – but also in many other countries. In Europe, French is spoken in Switzerland, Belgium and Luxembourg. They speak French in Quebec, a province of Canada, and in several countries of Africa. In the world there are 52 countries where French is spoken!

(b)
Au Maroc on	parle français.
Un pays où on parle	français est un pays francophone.
Le Québec est une	province du Canada.
On ne parle pas	français en Angleterre.
En Suisse on parle trois langues:	français, italien et allemand.

(c)   Nathalie veut une nouvelle robe.
Elle va au magasin avec son amie Sara.
Elle met quatre robes.
Sara aime la robe verte mais Nathalie préfère la bleue.
Nathalie décide: c'est la bleue!

Chapitre 8

Ma famille et mes animaux
Exercice 8.1 – CD:50

Hello! My name is Tochiko. I am 12 and I live in La-Roche-sur-Yon in the Vendée. It is a beautiful town which I love. Here's my family: my father, my mother, my sisters and my brothers. There are also my grandfather and grandmother. My parents are wonderful. They have five children. I have two sisters called Mina and Marie-Christine and two brothers called Georges and Olivier, who love sport. Marie-Christine (who is disabled) and I are adopted. I am of Japanese origin. Marie-Christine is 16. She loves art and music. Me too, I like music and I have a big collection of CDs. Our little sister Mina, who is 9, loves animals. She looks after our two cats.

1. Any eight facts about Tochiko's family deserve credit:

   She has two sisters: Mina and Marie-Christine.
   She has a mother and father.
   She has two brothers: Georges and Olivier.
   Tochiko and Marie-Christine are adopted.
   Marie-Christine is disabled.
   The family lives in La Roche-sur-Yon, in Vendée.
   It's a beautiful town, which Tochiko loves.
   Tochiko is of Japanese origin.
   Marie-Christine likes art and music.
   Mina loves animals.

2. (a) Tochiko habite à La Roche-sur-Yon.
   (b) La Roche-sur-Yon est en Vendée.
   (c) Marie-Christine adore le dessin et la musique.
   (d) Les frères de Tochiko adorent le sport.
   (e) Mina a neuf ans.

Exercice 8.2

1. Il s'appelle Jean-Paul.
2. Les grand-mères s'appellent Chantal et Marie-Claire.
3. Ils sont (*or, more correctly,* Ce sont) les frères de Tochiko.
4. Mina est la sœur de Tochiko.
5. Christine est la mère de Tochiko.

Exercice 8.3 – CD:51

Mina is at school with her friends. It is break. They are chatting.

Mina. So, you are from a large family?
Alice. Not like yours. Actually, how many of you are there?

Mina. There are seven of us at home. And we have our grandparents as neighbours!
Joséphine. That's incredible. Do you live in a big house?
Mina. Oh, yes. There are five bedrooms.
Alice. There are five of us at our home. I have two brothers.
Mina. I also have two brothers. The younger one wants to go into the police.
Joséphine. Your elder sister, what is she called?
Mina. She is called Marie-Christine.

1. She says there are seven.
2. Her grand-parents live nearby.
3. He wants to be in the police force.
4. There are five bedrooms.
5. She is Mina's older sister.

Exercice 8.4

1. (a) My uncle is my aunt's sister. (F)
   (b) My step-mother is my father's mother. (F)
   (c) My grandparents are my parents' parents. (V)
   (d) My cousin is the granddaughter of my uncle and aunt. (F)
   (e) My aunt is the sister of my father or mother. (V)

2. My name is Sonia. I have a brother who is called Guy and a sister who is called Marina. My parents are called Jean-Jacques and Sandrine. Mum's parents are Alphonse and Léopoldine, and my other grandparents are François and Marie-Claude. So, there we are!

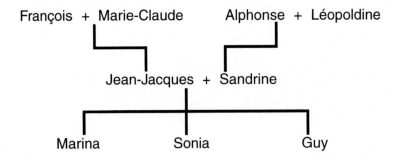

3. Suggested answer:

   Je m'appelle Jeanne. J'ai un frère qui s'appelle Philippe. Mes parents s'appellent Marcel et Claire. Les parents de mon père sont Jean-Paul et Marie, et mes autres grands-parents sont André et Anne.

4. Pupils are asked to write in French a letter to a friend, in which they talk about their family in as much detail as they can.

Exercice 8.5

In this exercise, pupils must respond to each picture orally or in writing, saying whether they have or do not have one of those animals:

e.g.   Moi, j'ai un chien à la maison.   I have a dog at home.
       Moi, je **n**'ai **pas de** chat à la maison.   I have **no** cat at home.

Check the practice of **pas de** ...

Exercice 8.6 – CD:52

Tochiko.   Hi, Philippe!
Philippe.   Hey! Tochiko. How are you?
Tochiko.   Fine. Do you have any animals at home?
Philippe.   I have a dog, but it's difficult.
Tochiko.   Why? Don't you like your dog?
Philippe.   Of course! I love animals, but my parents are divorced, so at home it's only my father and I.
Tochiko.   And your father, does he work?
Philippe.   Yes. So, it is not easy.

1.   She asks if he likes his dog.
2.   His father lives with him.
3.   It's not easy because it's only him and his father at home and his father works.

Les questions - CD:53

Examples of the three ways of asking a question are read out.

Exercice 8.7

1.   Do you like your school?
2.   Do the teachers speak English?
3.   Are we going to Paris this afternoon?
4.   Do you like my little village?
5.   Do you hate Maths?
6.   Do you live with your grandmother?
7.   Can you eat a *tartine*?
8.   Is Olivier going to his aunt's house?
9.   Are we arriving at Nantes at 1.00 pm?
10.   Does the train arrive in Paris at 2.00 pm?

Exercice 8.8

Answers may vary, depending on which method is used.

1.   Tu es français / française?
2.   Est-ce que tu habites en France?
3.   Aimes-tu l'école?
4.   Est-ce que les profs sont sympa?
5.   Tu manges des croissants? Et des baguettes?
6.   As-tu des animaux à la maison?
7.   Est-ce que tes amis aiment jouer au football?

8. Tu joues au tennis?
9. Est-ce que ta mère parle anglais?
10. Aime-t-elle la France / Est-ce qu'elle aime la France?

Exercice 8.9

Pupils use the pictures as prompts to ask questions orally to their partners. Here are some suggestions:

Est-ce que tu aimes les ordinateurs?	Do you like computers?
Tu as un chien à la maison?	Do you have a dog at home?
Qui fait la cuisine à la maison?	Who does the cooking at home?
As-tu beaucoup de livres dans ta salle de classe?	Do you have lots of books in your classroom?
Vas-tu à l'école en bus?	Do you go to school on the bus?
Ma sœur est toujours dans la salle de bains; et toi?.	My sister's always in the bathroom.; what about you?

Les verbes: écrire - CD:54

The irregular verb écrire, in the present tense, is read out.

Exercice 8.10

1.	Papa veut écrire à M. Duval.	Papa wants to write to M. Duval.
2.	Maman écrit à Jean-Luc.	Mum writes to Jean-Luc.
3.	Nous écrivons dans nos cahiers.	We write in our exercise books.
4.	Vous écrivez en français.	You write in French.
5.	Joséphine et Nicolas écrivent à leur tante.	Joséphine and Nicolas write to their aunt.

Exercice 8.11

1. Marie écrit à sa grand-mère.
2. Nous écrivons à nos correspondant(e)s.
3. J'écris dans mon cahier.
4. Ils écrivent une lettre à Nicolas.
5. Antoine et Françoise écrivent des lettres.

Exercice 8.12

1. Marie n'aime pas écrire à sa grand-mère.
   Marie doesn't like writing to her grandmother.
2. La soeur de François ne mange pas à la cantine de l'école.
   François's sister doesn't eat at the school dining room.

3. Nous ne rentrons pas à la maison.
   We don't go back home.
4. Antoine et Chantal n'écrivent pas aujourd'hui.
   Antoine and Chantal aren't writing today.
5. Tu ne peux pas regarder la télévision après le dîner.
   You cannot watch television after dinner.
6. Le frère aîné de Christine ne s'appelle pas Jérôme.
   Christine's elder brother's name isn't Jérôme.
7. Tochiko ne veut pas manger au restaurant ce soir.
   Tochiko doesn't want to eat at the restaurant this evening.
8. L'oncle de Jules n'est pas très poli.
   Jules's uncle is not very polite.

Exercice 8.13

Je ne suis pas anglais, je suis français. J'habite à Nantes avec mes deux frères et ma sœur. Nous avons deux chiens et un chat qui s'appelle Turc et qui a les yeux bleus.

I am not English, I am French. I live in Nantes with my two brothers and my sister. We have two dogs and a cat which is called Turc and which has blue eyes.

Exercice 8.14 – CD:55

The shops in Nantes are superb. There are some good shops in La Roche-sur-Yon, but I prefer Nantes because there is a bigger choice. For example, there is a shop in La Roche called 'Our Friends the Animals' where there are puppies and kittens and hamsters. In Nantes, there are dogs, cats, hamsters, but also guinea-pigs, birds, goldfish and many other animals.

Aurélie, 10 years, Belleville (Vendée)

1. Un petit chien
2. Un petit chat
3. Vrai
4. Nos Amis les Animaux

Exercice 8.15

Pupils discuss their families and their pets, as in the example.
   'How many of you are there in your family?'
   'There are three of us. My mother, my father and me.'
   'Do you have any animals?'
   'Yes. I have a dog and two cats.'

Vive la France! 8

(a) Pets are very important in France. There are all sorts of animals: dogs, cats, goldfish, birds, mice... According to a recent survey, there are 40 million pets in France!
(b) Les intrus: un chat; un oiseau. (All the rest are people).

Chapitre 9

On se retrouve!
Exercice 9.1 – CD:56

Paul.   So, what shall we do tomorrow?
Claire.   Er... Shall we go to the skating rink?
Maurice.   Oh, no. I don't like that. I am too tired.
Anne.   Shall we to to the cinema? There is a new James Bond film.
Paul.   Yes. Why not? Good idea.
Claire.   What time does the film begin?
Anne.   At eight o'clock, I think.
Maurice.   And which cinema is it at?
Anne.   At the *Concorde* in La Roche.
Paul.   Right then, where shall we meet?
Maurice.   At the bus stop at 7.30.
Paul.   Which bus stop?
Maurice.   In front of the Café des Sports. Rue des Acacias.
Paul.   Right. Fine. See you tomorrow!
Maurice.   See you tomorrow!

1.   The skating-rink
2.   A new James Bond film.
3.   8 p.m.
4.   Outside the Café des Sports.
5.   At 7.30 the following day.

À, au, aux - CD:57

Examples of the use of à, au. à l' and aux are read out.

Exercice 9.2

1.   Let's meet at the café.
2.   Paul and Maurice eat at the restaurant.
3.   There's a good film on at the Concorde cinema.
4.   Anne doesn't go to the church.
5.   Claire and Paul go to the Café des Sports.
6.   We're not going to the stables.
7.   There is a bus stop at the church.
8.   The film begins at 9 pm.
9.   Dad arrives at the airport at 4.30.
10.   He meets up with Mum in the park.

Exercice 9.3

1. On va au café.
2. On aime aller aux cafés.
3. Il donne le CD à son frère.
4. Elle parle aux frères de Claire.
5. Ils parlent à l'oncle de Philippe.
6. On se retrouve à la piscine?
7. Ils sont à l'arrêt de bus.
8. Tu vas au cinéma, Nicolas?
9. Nous allons (On va) au restaurant.
10. Elle reste à la maison.

Exercice 9.4

Pupils prepare and perform conversations based on the places in the pictures, as in the example:

'Where shall we meet?'
'At the swimming pool.'
'At what time?'
'At seven o'clock.'
'OK. At the swimming pool at 7.00. Goodbye.'

J'ai faim! - CD:58

Avoir faim, and the concept of idioms with avoir, are illustrated by the dialogue on the CD.

Exercice 9.5 - CD:59

Picture 1
Girl.   Hello.
Boy.   Hello. What's your name?

Picture 2
Girl.   I'm called Josette. What about you?
Boy.   My name's Daniel.

Picture 3
Girl.   What are you going to do?
Boy.   I'm going to go fishing.

Picture 4
Girl.   You're going to catch some fish?
Boy.   Yes. I'm going to catch some big fish.

Picture 5
Girl.   Let's have a look!
Boy.   See?

Picture 6
Girl.   Gosh! They're big!

Picture 7
(Later, at home...)
Girl.   There's a little boy called Daniel.
Mum.   Oh. Right.

Picture 8
Girl.   He's going to catch some big fish!
Mum.   Oh. Right.

Picture 9
Girl.   Daniel and I are going to look for snakes!
Mum.   Oh. Right.

1.   He says he's going fishing.
2.   The fish he wants to catch.
3.   There's a little boy called Daniel.
4.   She says 'Ah bon...', which means, 'Oh. Right.'
5.   She tells her they are going to look for snakes!

Exercice 9.6

1.   Je vais regarder la télévision.
2.   Elle va parler au garçon.
3.   Il va à l'église le dimanche.
4.   Il ne va pas à l'école le samedi.
5.   Elle ne va pas écouter.
6.   Est-ce que Daniel va à la piscine?
7.   Josette va chercher des serpents?
8.   Qu'est-ce que nous allons faire?
9.   Veux-tu aller au café?
10.   À quelle heure allons-nous manger?

Exercice 9.7

1. + (d)   Qu'est-ce qu'on fait après le petit déjeuner?
2. + (e)   On peut aller au restaurant?
3. + (a)   Tu veux aller à la piscine?
4. + (b)   Le fim commence à huit heures et demie
5. + (c)   On se retrouve à l'arrêt de bus.

Exercice 9.8

1.   au cinéma
2.   à la piscine
3.   au restaurant
4.   au théâtre
5.   aux magasins
6.   au centre sportif
7.   au café
8.   au parc
9.   à la patinoire
10.   au club

N.B. Pupils may need some help with Q.6 !

Exercice 9.9

1. À l'église.
2. Tu veux aller à la pêche?
3. Après l'école.
4. On se retrouve où?
5. On se retrouve.
6. À l'arrêt de bus.
7. Le film commence.
8. À quelle heure?

Exercice 9.10

1. Tu vas trouver le film très intéressant.
   You are going to find the film very interesting.
2. Nous allons regarder la télévision ce soir.
   We are going to watch television this evening.
3. Elle va manger à la maison avant le film.
   She is going to eat at home before the film.
4. Il va chanter avec le groupe de Jean-Paul?
   Is he going to sing with Jean-Paul's group?
5. Oui, je vais chanter avec le groupe lundi soir.
   Yes, I am going to sing with the group on Monday evening.
6. Maman va écouter la radio.
   Mum is going to listen to the radio.
7. Nous allons habiter à Paris.
   We are going to live in Paris.
8. Paul va donner un CD à Christine.
   Paul is going to give a CD to Christine.
9. Vous allez acheter une bicyclette?
   Are you going to buy a bicycle?
10. Oui. Nous allons acheter une bicyclette en ville.
    Yes. We are going to buy a bicycle in town.

Exercice 9.11

The odd one out is number 4: the others don't mention fruit!

Exercice 9.12

1. J'aime aller **au** restaurant quand j'ai faim.
   I like to go to the restaurant when I'm hungry.
2. On va tous les jours **à l'**école en voiture.
   Every day we go to school by car.
3. **Au** parc il y a toujours quelque chose à faire.
   At the park there is always something to do.
4. Je vais regarder un film **au** cinéma.
   I'm going to watch a film at the cinema.
5. Vous allez manger **au** café?
   Are you going to eat at the café?

6. On va écouter un bon concert **à la** radio.
   We are going to listen to a good concert on the radio.
7. On se retrouve **au** club de squash à 18 h.
   Let's meet at the squash club at 6.00 pm.
8. Nous allons **aux** magasins le lundi.
   We go to the shops on Mondays.
9. On va **à la** piscine samedi?
   Shall we go to the swimming pool on Saturday?
10. Non, je ne peux pas. Nous allons **à la** plage.
    No, I can't. We are going to the beach.

Vive la France! 9

(a) In 1515, they began the building of the Château de Chenonceau, on the banks of the Loire, one of France's main rivers. The châteaux of the Loire are magnificent. They are very often visited by the French, and by tourists from all over the world.

(b) Tu veux aller à un **concert** de musique?
Où **habites**-tu? Moi j'habite à Paris.
Quel **âge** as-tu?
On va à Paris par le **TGV**
Il y a un bon restaurant **en** ville.
On se retrouve **au** café?
La Loire est **un** fleuve.

(c) CHATEAU

(d) on the banks of = au bord de
one of the main rivers = un des fleuves principaux
they are very often visited = ils sont très fréquentés
in 1515 = en 1515

Chapitre 10

Les activités

Marcel. What do you do at home after lessons?
Philippe. Sometimes I draw, or I listen to CDs. What about you?
Marcel. Me, I play table tennis with my sister, or else I play tennis.

Exercice 10.1 – CD:60

Philippe. You play table-tennis with your sister?
Marcel. Yes. And tennis sometimes. It depends.
Philippe. And it's you who win?
Marcel. No! Well... not always!
Philippe. Shall we play tennis today?
Marcel. No I can't. I'm going to do my Latin this afternoon.
Philippe. Fair enough.
(on the telephone:)
Henri. Listen, Philipe. Do you want to come to my house with Marcel?
Philippe. Yes, I should really like to. But Marcel can't. He is going to do his homework.

1. Table tennis and tennis.
2. Not always.
3. He's doing his Latin.
4. It prevents him from playing tennis with Philippe.
5. That Philippe should come over with Marcel to his house.

Les verbes du 2e groupe (-IR) - CD:61

The verb finir, in the present tense, is read out.

Exercice 10.2

Any two of the following:

finir = to finish

je finis	nous finissons
tu finis	vous finissez
il finit	ils finissent
elle finit	elles finissent

choisir = to choose

je choisis	nous choisissons
tu choisis	vous choisissez
il choisit	ils choisissent
elle choisit	elles choisissent

remplir = to fill

je remplis	nous remplissons
tu remplis	vous remplissez
il remplit	ils remplissent
elle remplit	elles remplissent

punir = to punish

je punis	nous punissons
tu punis	vous punissez
il punit	ils punissent
elle punit	elles punissent

Exercice 10.3

1. Are you finishing your homework?
2. She chooses a cake.
3. We fill the glasses.
4. They punish the pupils.
5. We finish lunch.
6. She does not punish the girl.
7. We choose a present for Mum.
8. Fill my glass, please.
9. Aren't you choosing a CD?
10. I don't punish my dog.

Exercice 10.4

1. Il choisit un cadeau.
2. Je remplis ton verre.
3. Tu punis le méchant élève.
4. Elles finissent les devoirs.
5. On choisit le petit déjeuner.
6. Vous ne finissez pas vos devoirs.
7. Je ne choisis pas mon déjeuner.
8. Punit-elle les élèves?
9. Elles finissent les devoirs?
10. Tu remplis son verre.

Exercice 10.5

In this exercise, pupils are encouraged to say what they do after school in their free time. It is suggested that they use the opening dialogue of the chapter as a guide, along with the activity expressions on page 103.

Exercice 10.6

1. + (c) Pourquoi tu ne vas pas jouer au tennis ce soir?
   Why aren't you going to play tennis this evening?
2. + (d) Michel et Sonia font une promenade.
   Michel and Sonia are going for a walk.
3. + (b) Philippe joue au rugby.
   Philippe is playing rugby.
4. + (e) Je vais faire un tour de Paris.
   I'm going to go round Paris.
5. + (a) Après l'école je fais du vélo.
   After school I go cycling.

Exercice 10.7

1. Monsieur Blériot **joue** au tennis avec son amie.
   M. Blériot plays tennis with his friend.
2. Madame Colette **fait** une promenade.
   Mme Colette goes for a walk.
3. Nous **jouons** aux échecs après l'école.
   We play chess after shchool.
4. Nous allons **jouer** au rugby demain.
   We are going to play rugby tomorrow.
5. Ton prof **adore** faire du ski.
   Your teacher loves to go skiing.

Exercice 10.8

1. J'aime jouer au football.
2. Pauline adore nager dans la piscine.
3. Tu veux faire une promenade?
4. Nous allons faire du vélo.
5. Maman et papa n'aiment pas jouer au tennis.

Exercice 10.9

1. Je vais jouer au football.
2. Nous allons faire une promenade.
3. Vous allez jouer au rugby?
4. Elles vont faire du vélo.
5. On va jouer au tennis.

I'm going to play football.
We're going to go for a walk.
Are you going to play rugby?
They (f.) are going to go cycling.
We are going to play tennis.

Exercice 10.10

1. On va au cinéma demain.
2. Tu veux faire du vélo avec moi?
3. Mes parents vont faire une promenade après le déjeuner.
4. Mes amis vont jouer au tennis chez Michel.
5. Je ne vais pas jouer au football aujourd'hui.

Les verbes du 3e groupe (-RE) - CD:62

The verb vendre, in the present tense, is read out.

Exercice 10.11

Any two of the following:

rendre = to hand in / give back

je rends	nous rendons
tu rends	vous rendez
il rend	ils rendent
elle rend	elles rendent

descendre = to go down(stairs)

je descends	nous descendons
tu descends	vous descendez
il descend	ils descendent
elle descend	elles descendent

attendre = to wait for

j' attends	nous attendons
tu attends	vous attendez
il attend	ils attendent
elle attend	elles attendent

entendre = to hear

j' entends	nous entendons
tu entends	vous entendez
il entend	ils entendent
elle entend	elles entendent

vendre = to sell

je vends	nous vendons
tu vends	vous vendez
il vend	ils vendent
elle vend	elles vendent

répondre = to answer

je réponds	nous répondons
tu réponds	vous répondez
il répond	ils répondent
elle répond	elles répondent

Exercice 10.12

1. We don't wait for the bus here.
2. Can you hear? It's ten o'clock.
3. She goes down to the kitchen.
4. Monsieur Barreau sells his car.
5. Aren't you handing in your exercise book?

Exercice 10.13

1. Je vais rendre mon cahier après le déjeuner.
2. On descend à huit heures du matin.
3. Maman va attendre Philippe chez nous.
4. Sophie et Claire ne peuvent pas entendre la voiture.
5. Tu vends la maison, papa?

Exercice 10.14

1. Peux-tu jouer aux échecs avec Paul?
   Can you play chess with Paul?
2. Voulez-vous voir un film ce soir à la télé?
   Do you want to see a film this evening on t.v.?
3. Est-ce que Simone va au théâtre samedi soir?
   Is Simone going to the theatre on Saturday evening?
4. Fais-tu du cyclisme après les cours?
   Do you go cycling after lessons?
5. Est-ce qu'on peut jouer au rugby à l'école?
   Can you (we) play rugby at school?

Exercice 10.15 – CD:63

Philippe. So, you're finishing off your homework this afternoon, is that right?
Marcel. Yes. Afterwards, I'm going to Henri's.
Philippe. Brilliant! Have you still got my Banango CD?
Marcel. Er... Yes! I'll give you back your CD this afternoon!
Philippe. So, when are you going to finish, Marcel?
Marcel. I don't know.
Henri. I'm going to play football.
Philippe. Right OK.

Marcel does his Latin, but Philippe wants to go to play football at Henri's. Philippe goes to his friend's. He arrives at about 2.00 pm. Later, at 3.00 pm, Marcel finishes his homework, so he goes to Henri's and the three friends listen to a CD by a group called Banango. Later, they go out into Henri's garden where they play football. Marcel scores a goal. Philippe likes listening to CDs, but he prefers playing football. So does Henri!

1. He is finishing his homework.
2. That afternoon.
3. She hates them.
4. At about 2.00 pm.
5. They listen to the *Banango* CD, then play football.
6. Marcel scores a goal.

Exercice 10.16

Pupils may use the three pictures as a prompt for their answers to this question.

Vive la France! 10

(a) One of the pleasures of a visit to France is the cooking. At the restaurant and at home, the French like to eat well. When you go to France, it is preferable to appreciate the cooking of the region and to drink its wine. The French hate eating quickly: a meal is also an opportunity to chat and to relax as a family or with friends.

(b)   Des entrées = First courses
Des plats principaux = Main courses
Des fromages = Cheeses
Des desserts = Desserts

Notes

Notes